*Aerial view of Ennerdale and its lake from the summit of Angler's Crag (Stage 2)*

# THE COAST TO COAST WALK

The Coast to Coast Walk is an iconic 188 mile (302km) long-distance walk which crosses England from St Bees in Cumbria to Robin Hood's Bay in Yorkshire, traversing three National Parks as it goes. Usually tackled in a two-week stretch, occasionally over rugged and remote terrain, it is still within the reach of well-prepared novice backpackers.

### Contents and using this guide

This booklet of Ordnance Survey 1:25,000 Explorer maps has been designed for convenient use on the trail and includes:

- a key to map pages (page 2–3) showing where to find the maps for each stage.
- the full line of the walk with some variant sections
- an extract from the OS Explorer map legend (pages 99–101).

The companion guidebook, *The Coast to Coast Walk*, describes the full route from west to east (with summary route description east to west), alongside all that you need to plan a successful trip and lots of information about local history, geography and wildlife, and places to stay.

© Cicerone Press 2017
ISBN-13: 978 1 85284 926 9
Reprinted 2020, 2023 (with updates), 2021
Photos © Terry Marsh 2017

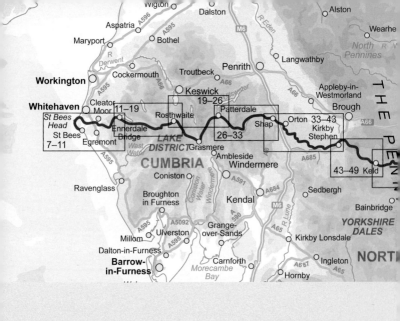

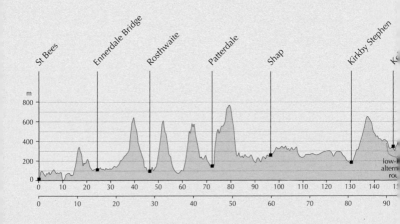

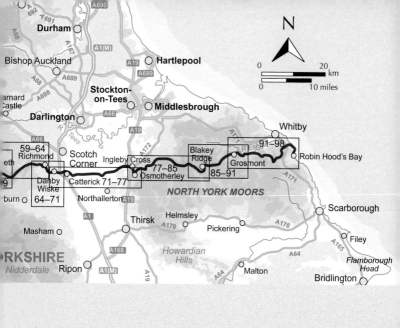

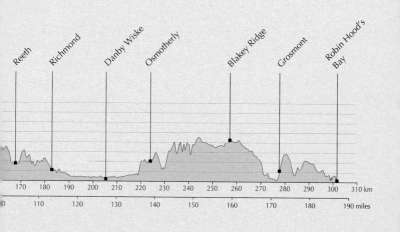

River Swale

# THE COAST TO COAST WALK

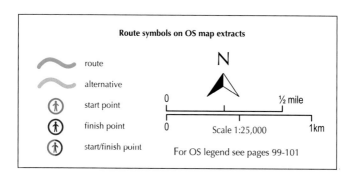

**Route symbols on OS map extracts**

～  route

～  alternative

🚶  start point

🚶  finish point

🚶  start/finish point

N

0                    ½ mile

0                          1km
          Scale 1:25,000

For OS legend see pages 99-101

Woodhouse

Minehouse West

St Bees Road

Bell House

Greenbank

High House

Air Shaft Far

Greenbank

Demesne

Thorney Beck

Wilson Pit Road

Lanehead

High Road

Byerstead

Townhead

Byerstead Road

MS

93

Midtown Farm

91

90

Poultry Farm

Disused Workings

Quarry (dis)

129

80

Sandwith

Croftfoot

Quarry (dis)

Quarry Bungalows

Sandwith Newtown

High House

Quarry (dis)

Hannahmoor Lane

126

117

Hannah Moor

100

Yarnflatt Hall

St Bees Lighthouse

Cloven Barth

**St Bees to Ennerdale Bridge**
**Start**       St Bees
**Finish**      Ennerdale Bridge
**Distance**    15 miles (23.9km)
**Time**        8hr

St Bees Head

Bowthorn Farm
Threapthwaite
86
93
97
Birks Farm
Ford
FB
79
Nor Beck
Brewery House
Birks House
A 5086
PO
89
Leconfield Industrial Estate
Keekle Grove
FB
Recn Gd
101
FB
15
71
Crossfield
71
Sch
PO
Wath Brow
High Wath
CLEATOR MOOR
Wath Grove
Mine (dis)
Low Farm
Blind Lane
Shaft (dis)
Sch
Low Wath
14
82
Cemy
Hotel
Ram's Gill
Rams Wo
FB
63
The Flosh
Hotel
91
CLEATOR M CP
Old Wood
90
Cleator
Sewage Works
Black How
Blackhow Wood
Long
Ehen Hall
Blackhow Bridge
Woodend
Row
84
Bragg Wood
rebank House
FBs
58
Longlands Lake
Nook Wood
200
Mine (dis)
Tips (dis)
Nook Farm
Quarry (dis)
Mine (dis)
Cobblehall
Dent Cottage
Co
Clints
Row Foot
Sunton Sike
150
Mine
Shaft
50

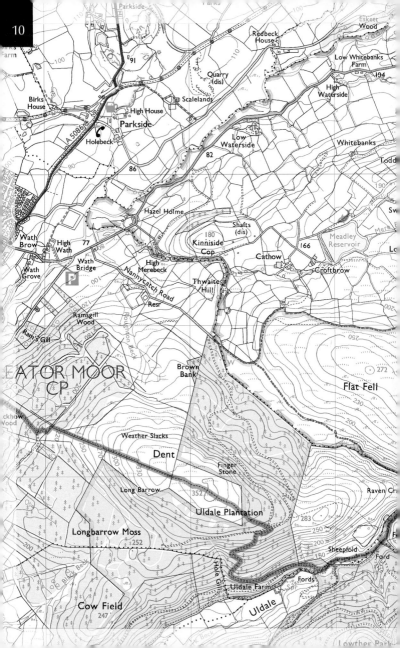

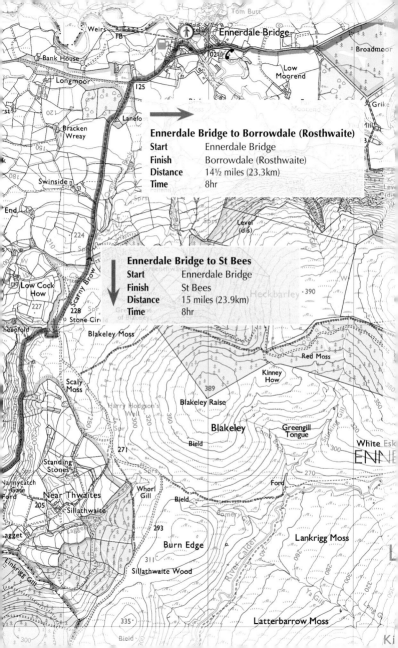

**Ennerdale Bridge to Borrowdale (Rosthwaite)**

| | |
|---|---|
| **Start** | Ennerdale Bridge |
| **Finish** | Borrowdale (Rosthwaite) |
| **Distance** | 14½ miles (23.3km) |
| **Time** | 8hr |

**Ennerdale Bridge to St Bees**

| | |
|---|---|
| **Start** | Ennerdale Bridge |
| **Finish** | St Bees |
| **Distance** | 15 miles (23.9km) |
| **Time** | 8hr |

How

FB

Fleet Gutter

Spr

How

Croftfoot

Howside

212

Whins

Woodfoot

Spr

150

How Hall
Farm

Ford

Beck

Spr

**Alternative route**

FB

Mir

Rothery Sike

Spr

Broadmoor

P

Grike

Weir

Weir

The Mill

FB

Bleach
Green
Cottages

Spr

Robin Hood's
Chair

Crag Farm
House

Anglers' Crag

Level
(dis)

Revelin Crag

Waterfall

Levels
(dis)

Crag Fell

523

522

Bield

Cairn 488

451

Level
(dis)

Grike

Mines
(dis)

Bield

Sheepfold

Moss

Black
Pots

Stinking Gill

Buck Hole

White Esk

# ENNERDALE AND KINNISIDE CP

491

Whoap

Sheepfold  Bield
Floutern Tarn
Gill Beck
Steel Brow
Sheepfolds
Level (dis)
Floutern Crag
Waterfall

**Herdus**

Cairn
Cairn
**Great Borne**

tenFarm
Cairn
.562
616
Shelter Cairn
Shelter Cairn

Sheepfold
Cairn
Scaw Well

Ford
16
Rake Beck
**Scaw**

Brown How
Sheepfold

Bowness
.333
**Bowness Knot**
270
Sheepfold

**Bowness Plantation**
280

erdale Water
200
Smithy Beck
Settlement

Latterbar
273

Nine Becks

Char Dub

Level (dis)
363
**Boat How**
Stair Knott

Boathow Crag
**The Side**
Mart Knott
FBs

Sail Hills

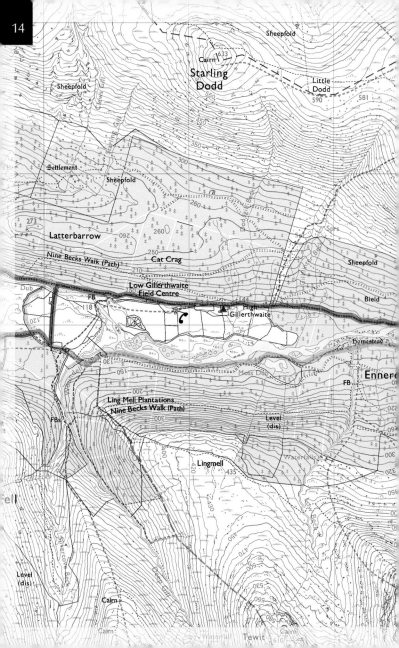

Sheepfold

Cairn 1633

**Starling Dodd**
560

Little Dodd
590

581

Sheepfold

Starling Gill

150

350

300

Dodd Beck

Spr

Settlement

Sheepfold

260

273

**Latterbarrow**
260

250

260

Sheepfold

Nine Becks Walk (Path)

**Cat Crag**

210

Low Gillerthwaite
Field Centre

Bield

Char Dub

FB
118

150

High
Gillerthwaite

120

Homestead

130

Moss Dub

FB

150

**Ennerd**

FBs

Ling Mell Plantations
Nine Becks Walk (Path)

200

300

Level
(dis)

300

Waterfalls

Lingmell
435

420

430

450

ell

470

Deep Gill

500

Level
(dis)

Cairn

520

550

560

580

Cairn

610

Tewit

Ling Comb

Dodd

Old Burtness

Burtness Wood

641 Cairns

The Saddle

Bleaberry Tarn

775

Pile of Stones

Red Pike

720

Chapel Crags

Cairn

700

White Pike

BP

High Stile

Standing Stone

806

BPs

Cairn

Grey Crag

The Knols

BP

Burtness Comb

500

Eagle Crag

Comb Beck

400

Raven Crag

Comb Crags

Sheepbone Buttress

300

White Cove

High Crag

744

Garn Edge

163

500

Forest

Marble Stone

400

River Liza

200

Sheepfolds

Ennerdale Fell Plantations

220

Fords

214

FB

White Pike

782

Pillar Rock

Pillar Cove

Robinson's Cairn

Raven Crag

Shelter

892

Hind Cove

Windgap Cove

Pillar

852

Pile of Stones

Farm

Weir

Peggy's Bridge
(FB)

Gatesgarth
Cottage

Meml

102

Low Crag

Fords

Low Raven
Crag

High Raven
Crag

Meetwith Edge

High Crag
Buttress

Sheepbone
Buttress

White
Cove

Buttermere Fell

Warnscale

High
Crag

High
Wax Knott

Low
Wax Knott

Warnscale Bottom

Gamlin End

CP Boy

Marble Stone

Ford

FB

Scarth Gap Pass

Cairn

Scarth
Gap

Seat

BPs

561

Hay Stacks

BPs
Path 597

582

Cairn

Green Crag

528

BPs

Innominate
Tarn

Dub's Quarry
(dis)

544

544

BPs

534

BPs

Raven Crag

Robinson's
Cairn

Hind Cove

Path

Ford

Black Sail
Hut

Seavy Knott

Proud
Knott

Ashcrag Holme

FB

Green
Cove

Looking
Stead

Ash Crag

269

Pile of Stones

Cloven Stone
Pile of Stones

587

Murt Rigg

Black Sail Pass

Boat
How

Kirkfell Crags

Pile of Stones

Gatherstone
Head

Baysoar

Boat How
Crags

Gatesgarthdale Beck

156

Moss Crag

Buckstone Hows

656

Maiden Stone

550

Yewcrag Quarries (dis)

500

Honister Crag

Black Star

etwith Pike

Burn Scarth

Wet Knotts

Honister Pass

Levels (dis)

Fox Fold

400

Honister Quarries (dis)

Quarry (dis)

Hopper Quarry (Slate)

Stang How

Bell Crags

332

Dismantled Tramway (Path)

Slate Mine

Wks

Honister Hause

Seatoller Fell

Level (dis)

Dubs Quarry (disused)

Drum House

Waterfall

Fleetwith

Sheepfold

Little Round How

Dubs Bottom

Mines (dis)

Great Round How

Waterfall

Grey Knotts

BPs

Raven Crag

398

Level (dis)

Seathwaite Slabs

Sourmilk Gill

BPs

Piles of Stones

BPs

Cairn

715

Brandreth

BPs

Gillercomb

Hanging Stone

Fawn Crag

Brin Crag

Moses Trod

Base Brown

Tongue

Cairn

646

Strawberry Gill

Gillercomb Head

BPs

610

BPs

Blackmoor Pols

BP

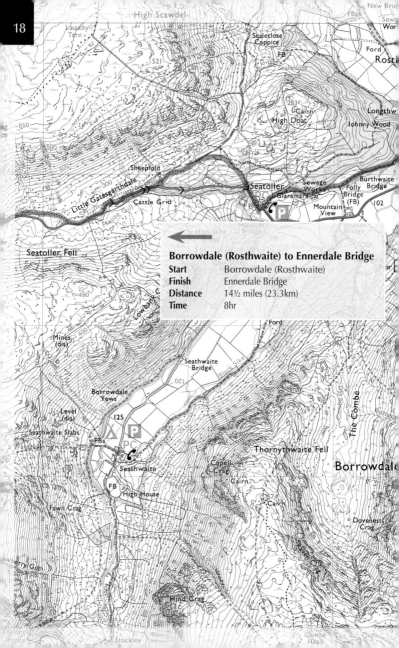

**Borrowdale (Rosthwaite) to Ennerdale Bridge**

| | |
|---|---|
| **Start** | Borrowdale (Rosthwaite) |
| **Finish** | Ennerdale Bridge |
| **Distance** | 14½ miles (23.3km) |
| **Time** | 8hr |

**Borrowdale (Rosthwaite) to Patterdale**

| | |
|---|---|
| Start | Borrowdale (Rosthwaite) |
| Finish | Patterdale |
| Distance | 15½ miles (25km) |
| Time | 9hr |

Deepdale

Cofa Pike

Fairfield

Mounds

Fairfield Brow

Brothers Parting Stone

Stepping Stones

Falcon Crag

Tarn Crag

Cock Cove

Cairns

Cairns

Grisedale Tarn

Hause Gap

Hause Moss

Rain Gauge

Hause Riggs

Cairns

Dollywaggon Pike

Post

Grisedale Hause

Cairn

Gavel Crag

Hause Riggs

850

830

574

CP Bdy

Cairn

Seat Sandal

736

720

Cairns

Cairn

Cairns

650

Triple Tongue

750

690

650

600

580

550

500

Willie Wife Moor

Raise Knott

Mine (dis)

Mine (dis)

Level (dis)

Homesdale Green

Ford Bridge

F.B.

F.B.

Pass of Dunmail Raise

MS

Raise

650

300

350

240

227

206

200

F.B.

M.S.

Dunmail Raise Pt (dis)

Dunmail Raise

Ash Crag

Cotra

Cotra Breast

Wythburn

Steel End

Stockhow Bridge

Pit (dis)

Sheepfold

1163

Grasmere

A 591

Stone Cove

Heron Pike

Blind Cove

Butter Crag

Riggs Crags

Stone Arthur

Level Hos

Brackenwife Knotts

Cairns

Rowan's Ground

Great Tongue

Ford

Winterseeds

Ford

Fords

Ford

Ford

Knott House Farm

Mill Bridge

High Broadrayne

FB

Pit (dis)

Travellers Rest

Michaels

Butharlyp Howe

Cem

Butharlyp Howe

River Rothay

Town Head

Helmside

Ghyll Foot

Low Raven Crag

High Raven Crag

Low Mill Bridge

Dale

Underhelm

Goody Bridge

Thorny How

Easedale Road

Ford

New Bridge

Helm Crag

White Crag

Lancrigg

Easedale

Easedale Beck

Gibson's Knott

Bracken House

Jackdaw Crag

Quarries (disused)

Brimmer Head Farm

Bield

Fords

James's Quarry (disused)

Deepdale C

Blake Brow

Blind Cove

Gavel Moss

Lord's Seat

Gavel Pike

Cairns

Isa Crag

Mossydale

Mart Crag

Erne Nest Crag

Greenhow End

The Cape

Cairns

Bannerside

Watch HI

The Step

Cairn

Plantade Lodge

St Sunday Crag

Hutaple Crag

Black Buttress

Hog Hole

Level (dis)

East Chockstone Gully

Y Gully

West Chockstone Gully

Grey Crag

Sheepfold

Cook

Cofa Pike

FB

Post

Deepdale Hause

Sleet Cove

Patterdale Common

FB

FB

Ruthwaite Lodge (Climbing Hut)

Griesdale Forest

Spout Crag

Brothers Parting Stone

Mine (dis)

Eagle Crag

Levels (dis)

Tarn Crag

Stepping Stones

Eagle Crag

Falcon Crag

Cairns

Grisedale Tarn

Caff Hole

Ruthwaite Cove

Cook Cove

Cairns

Nethermost Pike

Nethermost Crag

Post

High Crag

Cairns

Dollywaggon Pike

574

CP Bdy

Cairn

Fairfield

### Patterdale to Borrowdale (Rosthwaite)
**Start**      Patterdale
**Finish**     Borrowdale (Rosthwaite)
**Distance**   15½ miles (25km)
**Time**       9hr

### Patterdale to Shap
**Start**      Patterdale
**Finish**     Shap
**Distance**   15½ miles (25km)
**Time**       7–8hr

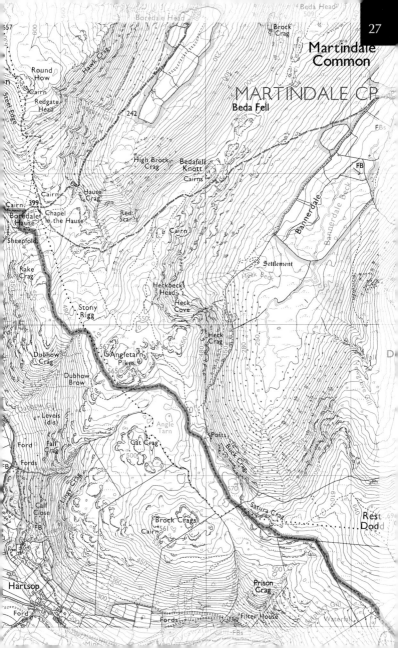

Boredale Head

Beda Head 509

Brock Crag

Martindale Common

MARTINDALE CP
Beda Fell

Round How
Cairn
Redgate Head
Steel Edge
Hawk Crag
242

FBs

FB

High Brock Crag
Bedafell Knott
Cairns

Bannerdale
Bannerdale Beck

Cairn 399
Boredale Hause
Chapel in the Hause
Hause Crag
Red Scar
Cairn

Sheepfold

Settlement

Heck Beck

Rake Crag

Heckbeck Head
Heck Cove

Stony Rigg

Heck Crag

Dubhow Crag
Angletarn Pikes
567

Dubhow Brow

Levels (dis)

Angle Tarn

Fall Crag
Gat Crag
500

Ford
Fords

Flag Crag

Posts
Buck Crag

Calf Close

FB

Brock Crags
Cairn 561

Satura Crag
570

Rest Dodd

Hartsop
Ford

Prison Crag

Fords

Filter House
Waterfall

FBs

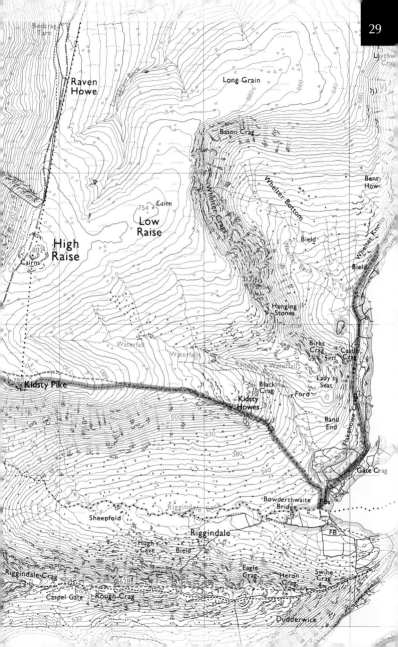

Redcrag Tarn

Raven Howe

Long Grain

Comb-in Beck

Bason Crag

Whelter Crags

Whelter Bottom

Langhow Crag

Bent Howe

Whelter Knotts

Bield

Bield

Cairn

754

Low Raise

High Raise

802

Cairns

Whelter Beck

Bield

Hanging Stones

Waterfall

Waterfall

Waterfalls

Randale Waterfall

Birks Crag

Castle Crag

Fort

Lady's Seat

Kidsty Pike

Black Crag

Ford

Kidsty Howes

500

430

380

340

Band End

Flakehowe Crag

Gate Crag

Bowderthwaite Bridge

FBs

Sheepfold

Riggindale Beck

Riggindale

FB

Hugh's Cave

Bield

Riggindale Crag

Eagle Crag

Heron Crag

Swine Crag

Caspel Gate

Rough Crag

530

Dudderwick

Littlewater • FB • Bield • Walmgate
Drybarrows • Littlewater • Eastward • 197
Pinnacle • Aika Hill • 282 • 260
Howe • Walmgate • 212 210 • 205 • Spr
Burn Banks • Head • Ford
Cairn • Thornthwaite • FB
Bield • Cairn • Hall
Naddle • Dam
FB • 216 • Gate • Thornthwaite
Homestead • 16 • 012 • Park Bridge
Ford • Tip • Burnbanks • 210 • Naddle Bridge
(dis) • Dam • Frith Wood
Weir • 238 • 020 • Frith
Wood • Crag • Cairn
Nook
Boat • Scalebarrow
House • Naddle • Knott
263 • Farm • Ros
• 395 • Cairn • Scalebarrow
Hugh's Laithes Pike • Ford • Tarn
(Cairn) • Ford
Low Forest • Ford
426 • 15 • Cairn • Ford • Swainsey
Cairn • 410 • Crag
Highfield • Minkside
Crag • Weir
e Forest
390 • Reservoir
st • Cairn • 370
• Harper • Bewbarrow
419 • Hills • Crag
• 410 • Merc Sike • 241
Chy • 14 • Swindale Foot Crag
• 420 • 380
Fords • 387 • Swin
Long Rigg • Foo
Woodhowe • Powley's Hill • Swindale
Moss • 474 • Mullender • Low
465 • 264 • Karelade
**Haweswater** • Hannah
**Nature Reserve** • Crag • FB • Dam
re Shaw • Cairn • Black • Truss Gap • Ford
503 • Crag • Park Bank
Thorny • 280 • Ford • Waire

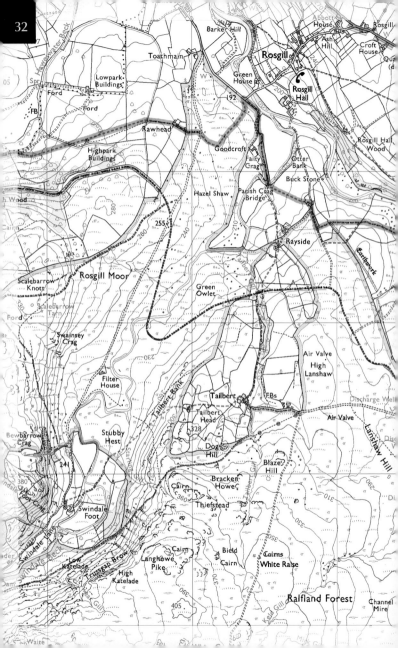

Brinns Farm

Crayston

289

290 Spr

285

Brinns Well

275 MS

257

290

The Edge

Thunder Stone

Sewage Farm

High Buildings

Skellaw Hill 260

New Ing Farm

**Shap**

Cemy

Abbey Wood

Stone

Tumulus

PO

F Sta

Sch

Goggleby Stone

309

315

**Shap to Patterdale**

| | |
|---|---|
| **Start** | Shap |
| **Finish** | Patterdale |
| **Distance** | 15½ miles (25km) |
| **Time** | 7–8hr |

Ruins of Abbey (Cistercian)

Stepping Stone

Ab Pa

256

270

300

Stone

MP

Keld

247 Chapel

SHAP CP

Cattle Grid

Ford

Keld Dub

Thornship

**Shap to Kirkby Stephen**

| | |
|---|---|
| **Start** | Shap |
| **Finish** | Kirkby Stephen |
| **Distance** | 20¾ miles (32.9km) |
| **Time** | 10hr |

Stepping Stones Ford

262

Brown Hill

Thornship Gill

Ford

Dam

276

Steps Hall

White Crag

Lingy Hill 252

Ford

Tewfit Mire

Discharge Well

Reamer Bank 280

Dam

Ford

Ullsmoor

Bridge

Quarry (dis)

Fall

Stone Circle 266

MP

Sprs

A6

Har

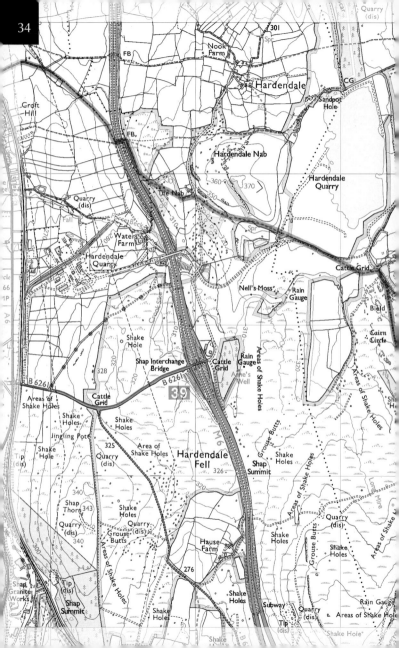

ROM

Settlement

Crosby Lodge

Long Cairn

**12**

Wicker Street

White Hag

Ford

old

Ford

Cairn

Ford

Bields

Stone Circle

Cairn

Crosby Gill

Sheepfold

Hollins Scar

Grouse Butts

Coalpit Hill

**Crosby Ravensworth Fell**

Shake Hole

**11**

Hazel Moor

Black Dub

Kings Well (Spring)

Grouse Butts

Robin Hood's Grave

**60**

**61**

**62**

ROMAN ROAD (course of)

**10**

Cairn

Grouse Butts

Cairn Howenook Pike

Bousfield Howe

Settlement

Quarries (dis)

Cattlehowe Quarry

Howe Nook

Meldikes

Quarry (dis)

Bullflatt

Thunder Stone

Quarry (dis)

Cattle Grid

303

Quarry (dis)

Quarry (dis)

Scarfoot Farm

**09**

282

Park

Dawns

254

Bowbrow

Quarry (dis)

Bousfield

MS

Park Lane

264

New House

Field Head

252

Mazongill

B 6261

243

B 6260

234

Quarries (dis)

**08**

Shake Holes

ROMAN ROAD (course of)

FBs

Gilts Bridge

Settlement

Gilts

Blasterfield
Farm

282

Cairns

Cattle
Grid

Hollin St
Cairn

Quarry
(dis)

319

Gaythorne Plain

344

307

Dina Gill

310

330

Bield

338

64

Quarry
(dis)

63

65

340

Howe
Robin

Quarry
(dis)

Thunder
Stone

378

379

343

BS

Orton Scar

Cairn  Mon

Beacon Hill

Quarry
(dis)

336

370

380

Cairn

National

Orton Scar

350

300
290

adfell

290

412

Cairn
Castle Fold
Settlement

270

Scar Side

273

Friar
Biggins

Knott

Cairns

280

FB

Spr

Scarside

Cairns

Street Lane

Spr

Resr

390

250

350

Raisbeck
320 Wood

300

orton

256

FB

Bland
House

Knott Lane

Stone Circle

260

Street

MS

250

250

B 6261 239

241

Howes

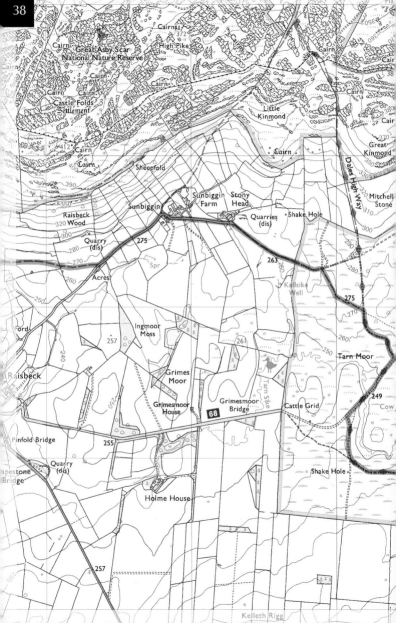

Burtree

Cowdale Slack

Cairn

Cairn

Grange Scar

Asket
Dub

323

Cattle Grid

Sheepdo

292

St Leonard's
Chapel
(remains)

Little Asby

Earthwork

Middle
Busk

Lousy Brow

308

Little Asby
Scar

356

Howes Well

Spear Pots

Cairn

339

Armaside
Wood

Sheepfold

Seavy Dub

Mazon Wath

247

Cattle Grid

266

260

250

250

Ford

Fell Head

W

271

271

280

Sunbiggin Tarn

273

290

300

310

Black
Rayseat

330

Rayseat

288

Grouse Butts

Mask Hill

Long Cairn

Great Ew

365

Rayseat
Pike

Rayseat Sike

279

Ford

Grouse Butts

301

Cattle
Grid

BS

Ewefell Mire

BS

309

Resr

BS

284

293

Ravenstonedale Moor

Dales High Way

301

Spr

Brackenber

Intake

Cairn

Tip
(dis)

Back Dub

Hard Rigg

Gracetemoor

Riggs

318

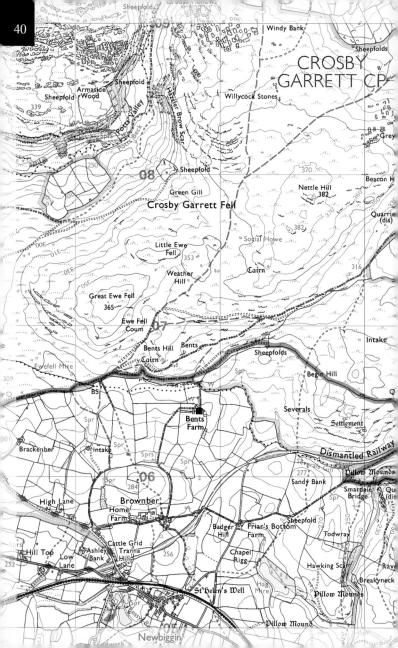

Tunnel

206 Oxenbrow Wood

Oxen Brow

Sheepfold

244

BS FB Ford

Chapel Well

Beck Lane

240

198

Hazel Gill

Mill Banks

Smardale Viaduct

284

Demesne Wood

220

Smardale Hall

School Lane

Smardale

224

235

Reservoir

240

236

Beck Wood

Smardale Demesne

Settlement

Smardale Intake

Tom Bank

ull Flat

270

260

Smardale Gill National Nature Reserve

WAITBY CP

Settlement

Smardale Gill

Settlement

Crag Wood

Witches Stride

gill

Pillow Mounds

Sheepfold

277

Limekiln Hill

Little Whitber

Grea Whitt

Smardale Fell

Sheepfolds Near Black Hill

Waitby Common

362

Tips (dis)

Sheepfolds

arry (is)

The Riggs

Burnt Bottom

Crawl Rigg

Sheepfolds

315

Pillow Mounds

Wether Hill

Wysack Well (Pond)

Quarries (dis)

298

Sheepfold Jervis Cross

Sour Hill

Lingy Intake

330

Rasett Hole

Slape Crag

Sheepfold

Thorny Pot Hole

350

Tumulus
377
Rasett Hill

Waitby Scar

High Wood

BS

344

Quarry (dis)

Ash Fell

Ash Fell Road

Shooting Butts

291

Quarries

346

KIRKBY STE

Wether Hill

Ford
176
166
Bu

FB
BS
Fond
Leases
Haber Hill
Riddlesay
189 · Hill
Riddlesay Hill

Barnskew
Hill
Far Leates Lane
173
Limekiln Hill
Enter

nskew
Wood
Stripes
Waitby Crossing
170
Moorlands

Smardale Mill
Grammary Bank
Bowber Hill
180

FB
Sandwath
Sandwath Sike

Oxenbrow Wood
A Beck
208
Sa
B

Oxen Brow
244
240
198
Spr

Waitby
Settlement
Waitby Gree Nature Rese

Mill Banks
Castle Hill
Spr
230

Beck Lane
School Lane
FB
Waitby Farm
Spr
Green Riggs

ate Hall
Smardale
224
235
Reservoir
Highmore Hill
267
Spr

236
Tom Bank
Waitby Intake
Kirkby Stephen Intake
In
Bo
Int

Smardale Intake
WAITBY CP
Settlements

Settlement
Wiseber Hill
Tumulus
Rest

Sheepfold
Quarry (dis)
Ben
Hil

Limekiln Hill
277
Little Whitber
Great Whitber
250
Midland Cottages
252
Kirkby Sta

dale Fell
362
Waitby Common
Sheepfolds Near Black Hill
290
A685
Petty Brow

Burnt Bottom
Crawl Rigg
Sheepfolds
315
Lane Head
Easegill Head

Sheepfolds
281
A683
Quarries (dis)

Wysack Well
Cairn

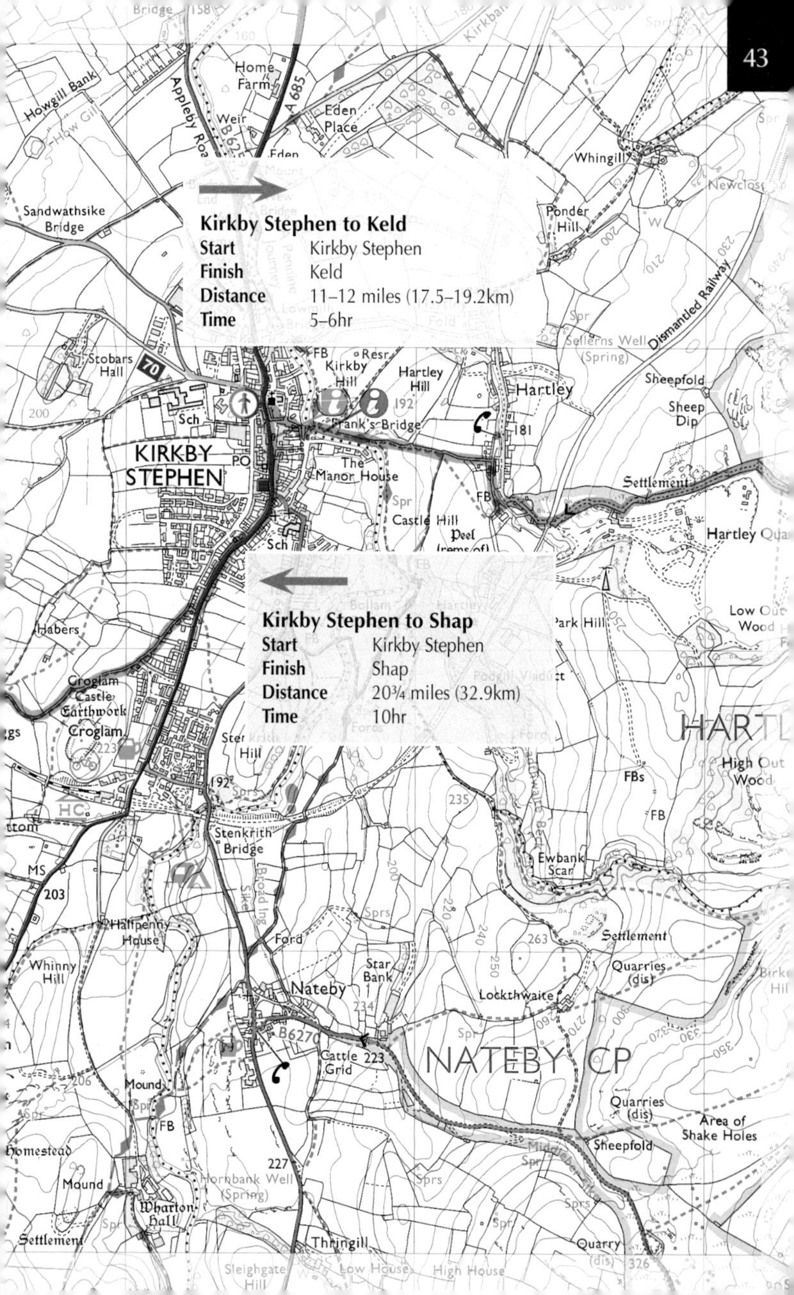

**Kirkby Stephen to Keld**

| | |
|---|---|
| Start | Kirkby Stephen |
| Finish | Keld |
| Distance | 11–12 miles (17.5–19.2km) |
| Time | 5–6hr |

**Kirkby Stephen to Shap**

| | |
|---|---|
| Start | Kirkby Stephen |
| Finish | Shap |
| Distance | 20¾ miles (32.9km) |
| Time | 10hr |

WIN

Sheepfold

Green
Fell

Gre

Workings
(disused)

Shafts
(dis)

Lines of
Shake Holes

Area of
disused Shafts

Little Longrigg Scar

Little Longrigg

Birkett Beck

Quarry
(dis)

Spr

Fold

Sheep
Dip

Quarry
(dis)

Settlement

Hartley Quarries

Quarries
(dis)

Fell
House

Shafts
(dis)

Sheepfold

Coalgill Sike

High Greyrigg

Middle Greyrigg

Low Out
Wood

Hartley
Ford

Hartley Beck

320

Hartley
Birkett

Shafts
(dis)

08

HARTLEY CP

High Out
Wood

352

Birkett
Hill 405

Needless Sike

Low Greyrigg

460

Shaft
(dis)

Shake Holes

Sheepfold

430

450

FBs

FB

Workings
(disused)

Shafts
(dis)

Shafts
(dis)

Riggs

Hartley Fell

Birkett
Hill 383

Ladthwaite

07 Reigill

Sheepfold

Area of Disused
Shafts and Pits

Shee

ttlement

Quarries
(dis)

Shafts
(dis)

Shake
Holes

Swallow
Hole

Quarries
(dis)

Area of
Shake Holes

350

Low
Dukerdale

Shafts
(dis)

Shee

efold

Nateby
Cow Close

06

High
Dukerdale

Dukerdale

326

Blind Gill
Holes

Swallow
Holes

Pits
(dis)

514

terbers
Hills

Butterbers

Seave Rigg

Sheepfold

Sheepfold

Sheepfold

Dukerdale Beck

Shah

Area of
Shake Holes

epfold

Pits
(dis)

458

Tailbridge
Hill 547

Nateby
Common

ew Cow
Close

401

Great Edge

Cairn

Lines of Shake Holes

Areas of
Shake Holes

Dukerdale

Pits
(dis)

Tailbridge

Pits
(dis)

Lamps

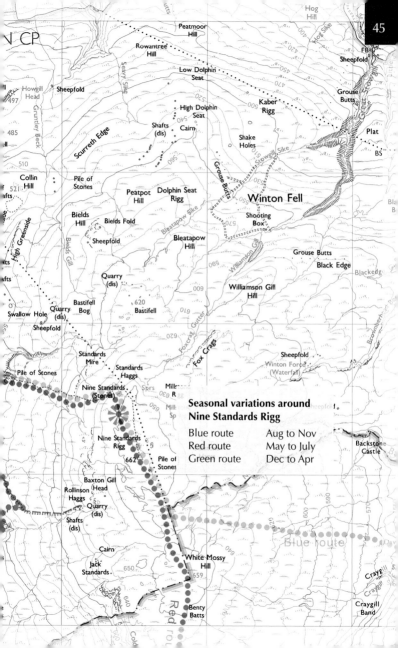

### Seasonal variations around Nine Standards Rigg

| | |
|---|---|
| Blue route | Aug to Nov |
| Red route | May to July |
| Green route | Dec to Apr |

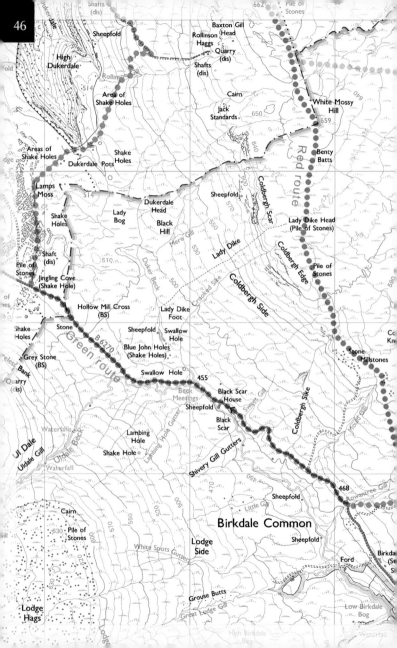

Shafts
(dis)

Baxton Gill
Head

Rollinson
Haggs

Quarry
(dis)

Shafts
(dis)

Sheepfold

High
Dukerdale

514

Rollinson Gill

Area of
Shake Holes

Cairn

Jack
Standards

650

White Mossy
Hill

659

Red route

Benty
Batts

Areas of
Shake Holes

Dukerdale Pots

Shake
Holes

Lamps
Moss

514

Dukerdale
Head

Sheepfold

Coldbergh Scar

Lady Dike Head
(Pile of Stones)

Shake
Holes

Lady
Bog

Black
Hill

Mere Gill

Coldbergh Edge

Shaft
(dis)

510

Duker Beck

500

Lady Dike

Coldbergh Side

Pile of
Stones

Pile of
Stones

Jingling Cove
(Shake Hole)

Crooked Sike

Hollow Mill Cross
(BS)

Lady Dike
Foot

Shake
Holes

Stone

B 6270

Sheepfold

Swallow
Hole

Green route

Blue John Holes
(Shake Holes)

Stone
Millstones

Grey Stone
(BS)

Wold Gill

Quarry
(dis)

Swallow Hole

455

Beck
Meetings

Black Scar
House

Coldbergh Sike

Sheepfold

Black
Scar

Ul Dale

Uldale Gill

Lambing
Hole

Shake Hole

Lambing Hole Gutter

Shivery Gill Gutters

Sweet Sike

Waterfalls

Waterfall

468

Lowantree Gill

Sheepfold

Birkdale Common

Cairn

630

Pile of
Stones

White Spots Gutter

Lodge
Side

Sheepfold

Ford

Birkda

Low Birkdale
Bog

Lodge
Hags

Grouse Butts

Great Lodge Gutter

High Birkdale
Bog

Waterfall

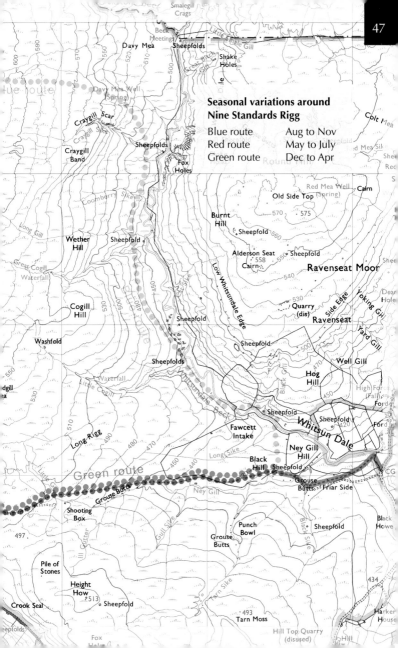

**Seasonal variations around Nine Standards Rigg**

Blue route     Aug to Nov
Red route      May to July
Green route    Dec to Apr

**Keld to Kirkby Stephen**
**Start** Keld
**Finish** Kirkby Stephen
**Distance** 11–12 miles (17.5–19.2km)
**Time** 5–6hr

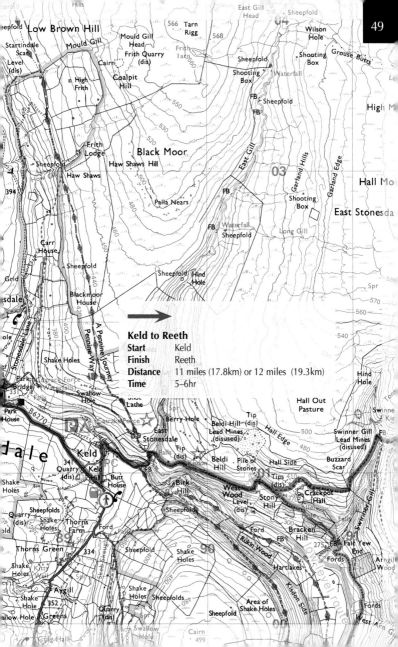

**Keld to Reeth**

| | |
|---|---|
| **Start** | Keld |
| **Finish** | Reeth |
| **Distance** | 11 miles (17.8km) or 12 miles (19.3km) |
| **Time** | 5–6hr |

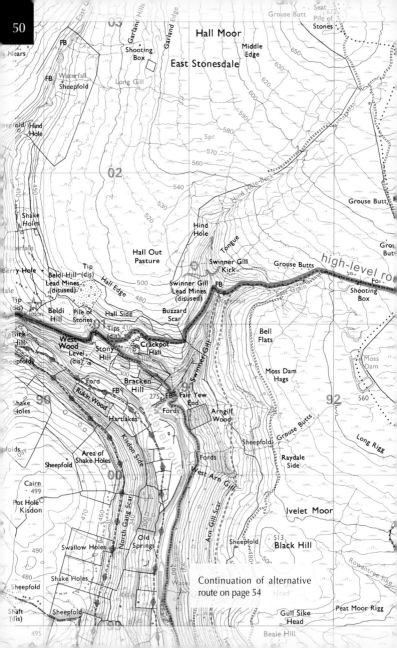

Continuation of alternative route on page 54

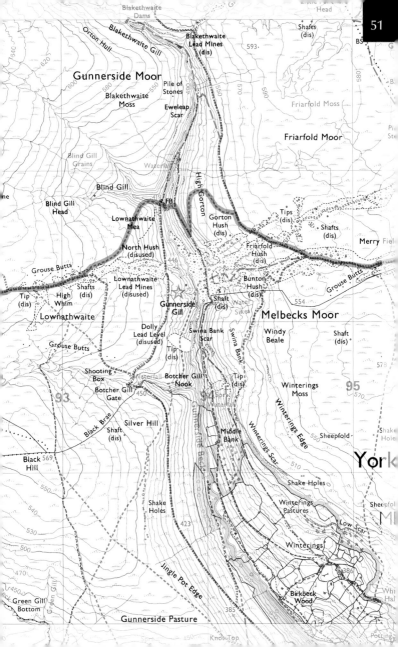

Blakethwaite
Dams

Blakethwaite Gill

Orton Hull

Blakethwaite
Lead Mines
(dis)

593

Shafts
(dis)

BS

## Gunnerside Moor

Blakethwaite
Moss

Pile of
Stones

Eweleap
Scar

Friarfold Moss

## Friarfold Moor

Blind Gill
Grains

Waterfall

High Gorton

Blind Gill

FB

Blind Gill
Head

Lownathwaite
Mea

Gorton
Hush
(dis)

Tips
(dis)

Shafts
(dis)

Merry Fiel

North Hush
(disused)

Friarfold
Hush
(dis)

446

Grouse Butts

Lownathwaite
Lead Mines
(disused)

Bunton
Hush
(dis)

554

Grouse Butts

Tip
(dis)

Shafts
(dis)

High
Whim

Gunnerside
Gill

Shaft
(dis)

Water
Sike

## Melbecks Moor

Lownathwaite

Grouse Butts

Dolly
Lead Level
(disused)

Swina Bank
Scar

Tip
(dis)

Swina Bank

Windy
Beale

Shaft
(dis)

Shooting
Box

Waterfall

Botcher Gill
Nook

Tip
(dis)

Winterings
Moss

95

578

Botcher Gill
Gate

450

Winterings Scar

570

Black Brae

Silver Hill

Shaft
(dis)

Middle
Bank

Winterings Edge

Sheepfold

Shake
Hole

93

Black
Hill

569

550

## York

530

500

Shake
Holes

423

Shake Holes

510

Winterings
Pastures

560

Low Scar

Sheepfol

MI

Green Gill
Bottom

Green Gill

470

450

Jingle Pot Edge

385

Winterings

386

Birkbeck
Wood

Whi
Ha

Potting

## Gunnerside Pasture

Knot Top

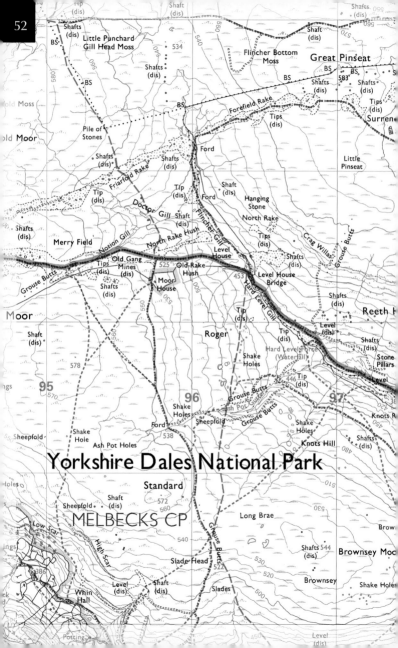

Shafts (dis)

Little Punchard Gill Head Moss

BS

BS

534

Shafts (dis)

Flincher Bottom Moss

Great Pinseat

BS

Shafts (dis)

583

Shafts (dis)

BS

Surren

Forefield Rake

Tips (dis)

Pile of Stones

old Moss

old Moor

Shafts (dis)

Ford

Little Pinseat

Friarfold Rake

Tip (dis)

Tip (dis)

Shafts (dis)

Shaft (dis)

Ford

Hanging Stone

Doctor Gill

Shaft (dis)

North Rake

Flincher Gill

Shafts (dis)

Merry Field

Norton Gill

North Rake Hush

Tips (dis)

Crag Willas

Grouse Butts

Grouse Butts

Level House

Shafts (dis)

Tips (dis)

Old Gang Mines (dis)

525

Old Rake Hush

453

Level House Bridge

Moor House

Shafts (dis)

Hard Level Gill

Shafts (dis)

Reeth

Moor

Shaft (dis)

Roger

Tip (dis)

Tip (dis)

Level (dis)

Shafts (dis)

578

Shake Holes

Hard Level Force (Waterfall)

Stone Pillars

**95**

570

**96**

146

Tip (dis)

**97**

Level

Shake Holes

Grouse Butts

Ash Pot Holes

Knots R

Ford

Sheepfold

Grouse Butts

Shake Holes

538

Shake Hole

Ash Pot Holes

Knots Hill

Shafts (dis)

Sheepfold

# Yorkshire Dales National Park

Standard

Holes

Shaft (dis)

572

Sheepfold

560

## MELBECKS CP

Low Scar

High Scar

540

Long Brae

510

530

386

Slade Head

Grouse Butts

522

520

Shafts (dis)

544

Brownsey Moo

Whin Hall

Level (dis)

Shaft (dis)

Slades

500

Brownsey

Shake Holes

Brow

Potting

Level (dis)

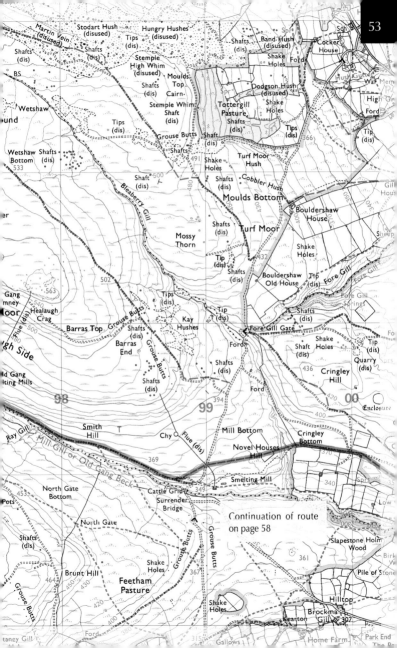

Martin Vein (disused)
Stodart Hush (disused)
Hungry Hushes (disused)
Tips (dis)
Tips (dis)
Band Hush (disused)
Shafts (dis)
Shake Holes
Cocker House
Ford
Hush Gutter
War Mem
Sch
BS
Shafts (dis)
Shafts (dis)
Stemple High Whim (disused)
Moulds Top Cairn
Dodgson Hush (disused)
Shake Holes
High Gr
Ford
Wetshaw
Shafts (dis)
Stemple Whim Shaft (dis)
Tottergill Pasture
Shafts (dis)
Tips (dis)
Tip (dis)
und
Tips (dis)
Shaft (dis)
366
Wetshaw Bottom
Shafts (dis)
Grouse Butts
Shafts
Shaft (dis)
Turf Moor Hush
533
491
Shake Holes
Cobbler Hush
Shaft (dis)
500
Shafts (dis)
Moulds Bottom
Bleaberry Gill
480
430
Bouldershaw House
Shafts (dis)
Turf Moor
Sheep
er
Mossy Thorn
437
Shake Holes
563
502
Tip (dis)
Boulershaw Old House
Tip (dis)
Fore Gill
Fore Gill
Gang mney Moor
540
Shafts (dis)
Fore Gill Springs
Fo
Healaugh Crag
500
Grouse Butts
Tips (dis)
Tip (dis)
Barras Top
Kay Hushes
Tip (dis)
Shafts (dis)
Fore Gill Gate
Shafts (dis)
Tip (dis)
gh Side
Barras End
Ford
Shake Holes
Quarry (dis)
d Gang lting Mills
Grouse Butts
Shaft (dis)
436
Cringley Hill
Shafts (dis)
Shafts (dis)
Ford
420
00
98
99
394
400
Enclosure
Ray Gill
Smith Hill
Chy
Flue (dis)
Mill Bottom
Cringley Bottom
370
Mill Gill or Old Gang Beck
369
Novel Houses Hill
Spr
453
North Gate Bottom
Cattle Grid
349
Surrender Bridge
Smelting Mill
340
Low
ots
North Gate
Continuation of route on page 58

Slapestone Holm Wood
Shafts (dis)
Shake Holes
361
Grouse Butts
Grouse Butts
Pile of Stones
Brunt Hill
464
450
430
Feetham Pasture
367
Birk
W
Hilltop
307
Brockma Gill
Grouse Butts
420
Shake Holes
Kearton
Home Farm
Park End The R
taney Gill
Ford
315
Gallows

54

Continuation of route on page 51

Black
Hill 569

Green Gill
Bottom

Jingle Pot Edge

Shake
Holes

Shake Holes

Winterings
Pastures

Low Scar

Sheepfold

ME

Winterings

Birkbeck
Wood

Whir
Hall

Pottin

Ford

Gunnerside Pasture

Knot Top

Pit
(dis)

Copper
Brae

Sun Side
Ford

Shake
Holes

Ford

Resr

Shake
Holes

Waterfall

Grains Gill

Ellas's Stot
Wood

Spr

Kisdon Bottom

Shoregill Head    Dyke Heads

Dyke
Heads

Gree

Gunnerside
Lodge

Cattle Grid

Gunn

Ivelet Heads

Ivelet

Marble
Scar

Sheepfold

Gunnerside
New Bridge

Sch

River Swale

Satron

237

Ivelet
Bridge

Mill Bridge

Sheepfolds

Cattle
Grid

248

B 6270

Lousy Hill

242

Waterfalls

Low
Oxnop

Oxnop
Bridge

Pennine Journey

Heugh

Shake Holes

Shake Holes

Satron Hangers

Kearton's
Wood

Swallow
Hole

Satron Side

Low Hai

Sheepfo

Low Walls

Tewit Mires

High Hangers

Gill Head

Ned Gate

Rash Gill

235

Shake Holes

Satron High Walls

Shafts
(dis)

Lead Mines
(disused)

Swallow Hole

Grouse
Butts

Castle
How 368

Spout Gill

Sheepfold

Hill Top

Shake
Holes

Shafts
(dis)

Keld Springs Edge

537

High
Oxnop

Tute
Hill

Swallow Hole  379

Jenkin
Gate

Oxnop
Ghyll

Shake Holes

Continuation of route on page 55

Potting

Ford

White Hill

Friar Folds Hill

405

450

430

Level (dis)

Shafts (dis)

Brownsey House Spr

Sprs

Bents

Waterfall

343

Barf End

Waterfall

Barf End Gate

432

Stoops Rigg

Sheepfold

410

400

Low Row Pasture

Barf

Shake Holes

Shake Holes

Lodge Green

Snaw House

Heights

350

Staney Gill Quarry (dis)

Ford

Little Rowleth Wood

300

400

Sch

PC

Gunnerside

248

Great Rowleth

Barf Side

221

Gunnerside Bottoms

250

225

Rowleth Wood

Smarber

137

Gunnerside New Bridge

Strands

Spr

205 Rowleth Wath

Cattle Grid

Hag Wood

Dubbing Garth

Sheepfold

Quarry (dis)

275

Lane

Hav H

Birk Hill

Spring End

Bank Heads

Low Hangers

Grave

Juniper Rigg

300

Muddy House Wat

Satron Hangers

Sheepfold

Shake Holes

Swallow Hole

330

350

Sheepfold

Nettlebed

256

Spr

High Hangers

Rigg Slack

Dover Hill

Tewit Mires

Flask Well (Spring)

Level (dis)

Crackpot

272

Ned Gate

North Gate

Spr

North Gate Scar

The Ings

318

Gill Plantation

Swallow Hole

Grouse Butts

530

Shafts (dis)

500

466

Levels (dis)

537

Blea Barf

540 Cairn

450

Crackpot Side

420

400

Harker Bridge

ngs Edge

520

530

Crackpot Moor

Sun Gate

Sun Side

370

380

Held Springs

Spr

Sheepfold

Little Bull Head

Shake Holes

Bloody Vale

Croft Beck

322

Summer Lodge

355

Summer Lodge Pasture

448

Tongue

Sheepfold

Swallow Hole

Dry Gill

Bracken Holes

Shafts (dis)

Sheepfold

Scurvy Scar

Shake Holes

Swallow Holes

Bull

Tarn Sike

Cave

418

Shafts (dis)

Beacon

Scar Brow

Shafts (dis)

Grouse Butts

Hog Gill

Summer Lodge Moor

Shafts (dis)

Grouse Butts

Dike Nick

Tarn Brow

Hog Gill Hole

Shafts (dis)

Summer Lodge Tips (dis)

Tarn

477

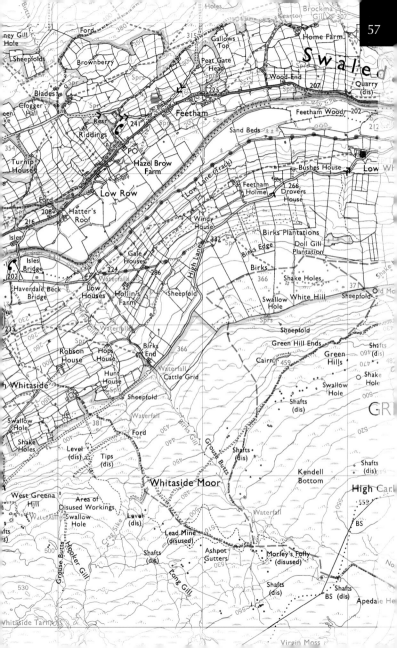

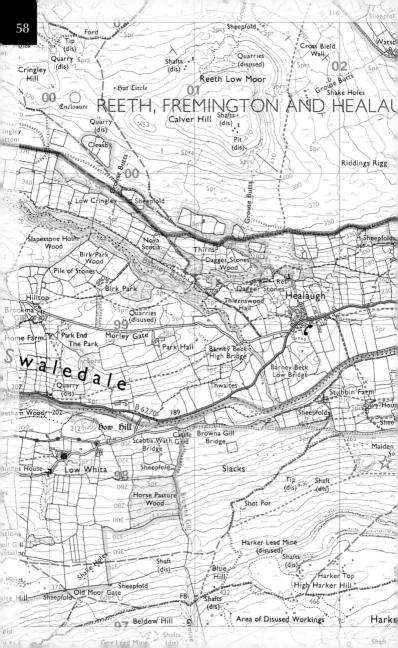

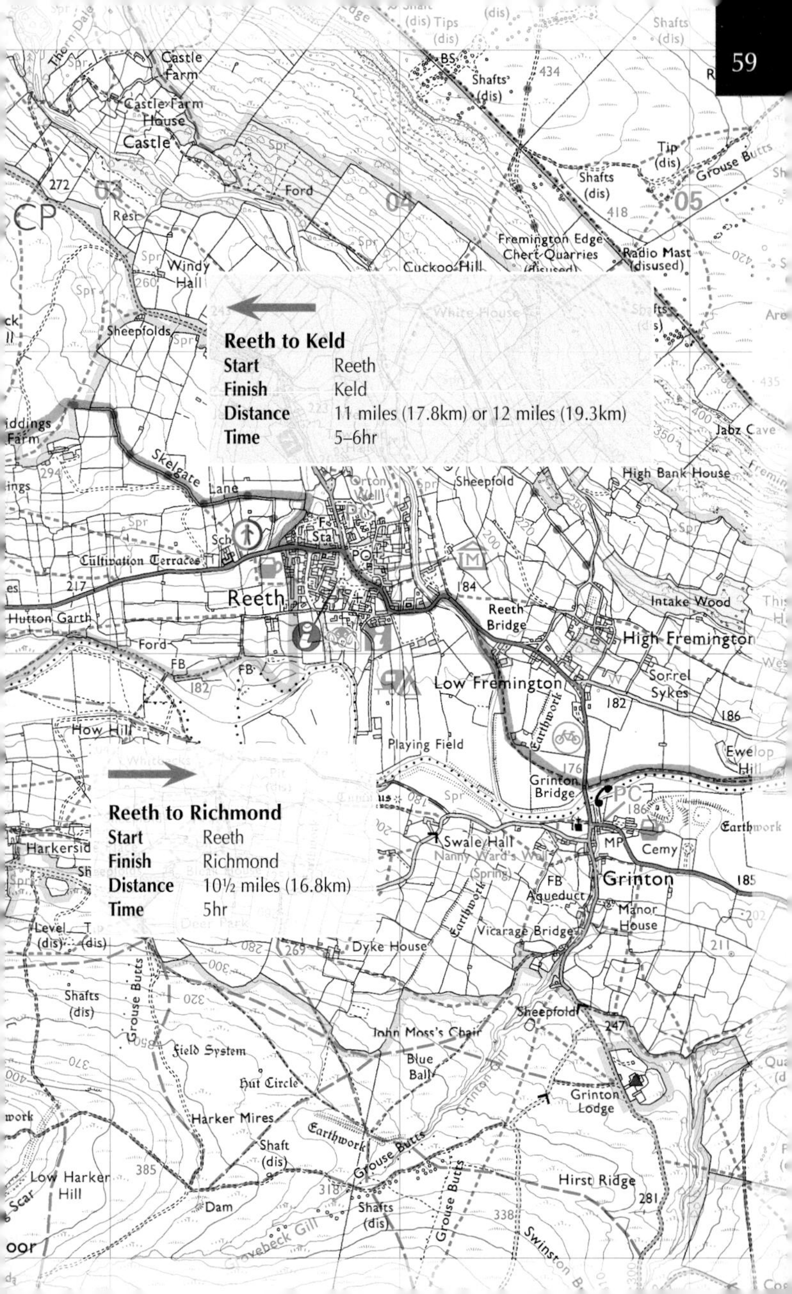

**Reeth to Keld**

| | |
|---|---|
| Start | Reeth |
| Finish | Keld |
| Distance | 11 miles (17.8km) or 12 miles (19.3km) |
| Time | 5–6hr |

**Reeth to Richmond**

| | |
|---|---|
| Start | Reeth |
| Finish | Richmond |
| Distance | 10½ miles (16.8km) |
| Time | 5hr |

Raygill Allotment

Ray Gill

Shafts (dis)

Stelling Spring

309

315

Helwith Road or G

Shafts (dis)

Fort

Tip (dis)

Grouse Butts

05

Marrick Moor

Shafts and Tips (disused)

Copperthwaite Allotment

Tip (dis)

Stelling Road

Spr

06

380

400

410

420

07

Grouse Butts

Shafts (dis)

327

Lower Stelling Farm

324

Radio Mast (disused)

418

Shafts (dis)

Area of Disused Shafts

Shafts (dis)

Grouse Butts

386

Shafts (dis)

309

Stelling

Musg

435

400

350

430

Jabz Cave

High Bank House

Fremington Edge

Spr

Shaft (dis)

Quarries (disused)

Buska

Quarries (disused)

Marrick Moor House

Intake Wood

Sheepfold

Thistle Hill

New Close Bank

324

Quarry (dis)

High Fremington

West Haggs

Reels Head

Quarry (dis)

314

Shafts (dis)

Quarry (dis)

Shafts (dis)

Sorrel Sykes

182

186

W

The Hagg

224

Reels Head Farm

Quarry (dis)

334

333

Ewelop Hill

Stony Bank Plantation

Shafts (dis)

Garnless Scar

Marrick Barf

Shaft (dis)

Shaf

Grinton

Earthwork

Cemy

186

Colt Park Wood

Sheepfold

Ince Wood

Garnless Wood

290

341

Garnless Scar

185

Minor House

202

211

River Swale

175

180

200

250

330

Spr

247

Cogden Hall

Sheepfold

B 6270

Mill Dam

Remains of Priory (Benedictine Nuns)

Steps Wood

Marrick Priory

Ford

Wood House

Quarry (dis)

Pits (dis)

Cogden Wood

090

MP

Stolerston Stile

BS

Sprs

71

Earthwork

Spr

on Edge

Pits (dis)

338

BSs

191

281

Shaft (dis)

BS

Stolerston Wood

Hags Gill Farm

220

188

Ridge

Shafts (dis)

Cogden Heugh

Spr

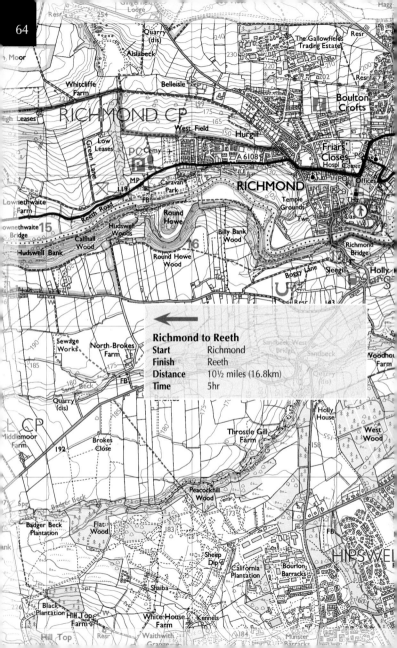

**Richmond to Reeth**

| | |
|---|---|
| Start | Richmond |
| Finish | Reeth |
| Distance | 10½ miles (16.8km) |
| Time | 5hr |

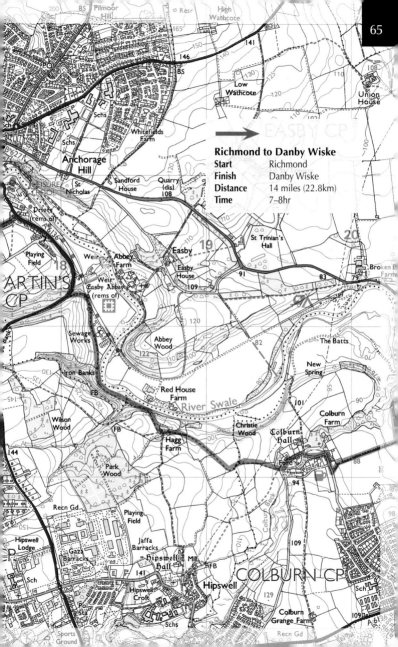

### Richmond to Danby Wiske

| | |
|---|---|
| **Start** | Richmond |
| **Finish** | Danby Wiske |
| **Distance** | 14 miles (22.8km) |
| **Time** | 7–8hr |

atherley

Rosey
Hill

**23**

Sand and
Gravel Quarry

**24**

Settling Ponds

Quarry

Elmfield
Hall

Banks
Lane

**25**

Bec
Brid

Homes
Farm PO

Citadilla

**69**

**64**
Hollow
Banks

Howe Hill Lane

Howe
Hill

**62**

Tancred
Grange

B 6271

Sch

Cemy

Catterick Bridge

MP

FB

Field House

**55**

Sand &
Gravel
Pit

Settling
Pond

**57**

**56**

Flat Lane

**56**

Bolt

**52**

CATARACTONIVM
ROMAN TOWN
Race Course

Sand & Gravel
Pit

Leeming Lane

**61**

Back Lane

**50**

P

Bolton-on-Swale Lake

Dere Street
ROMAN ROAD
(course of)

A 6055

Tel Ex

War Mem'l

Quarry

Sch

Cemy

**5**

**Catterick**

Sewage
Works

Brough Beck

Ellerton Pa

Manor
House

Balancing
Pond

Oran Lane

Marne
Barracks

Sewage
Works

ugh Beck

**70**

**66**

Hill

Quarry
(dis)

High Cowstand
Bridge

**63**

Low Cowstand
Farm

Cowstand
Farm

A 6055

Bainesse

A 6

**49**

spect

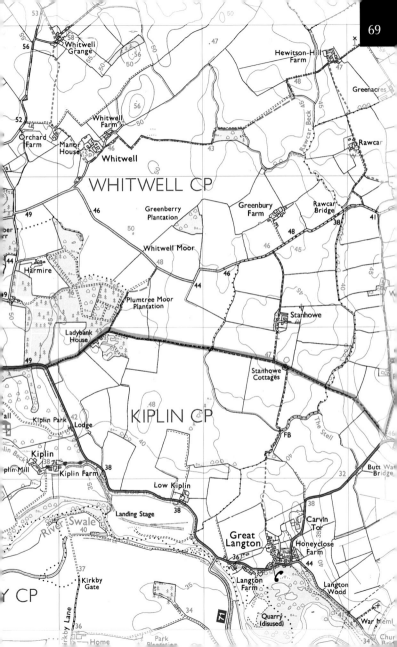

Tile House

Black Bridge

00

Danby Plantation

Fellgill Farm

41

Nigh-no-place

Greenacres

46

Fellgill Moor

46

Fellgill Covert

50

57

Hun

Rawcar

50

Spencer Close

44

99

46

Nurseries

42

West Farm

Rawcar Bridge

38

41

Streetlam

High-Moor

45

Streetlam Farm

48

45

Hanstead

40

Streetlam Whin

Mid Fa

Low Brockholme

45

White House Farm

50

50

44

DANBY WISK

98

46

Moor House

50

Brockholme Farm

38

Red House

Brockholme

GREAT LANGTON CP

43

47

High Brockholme

46

B 6271

43

Butt Wath Bridge

97

Langton Grange

32

52

48

Mossa Gr

41

Carvin Tor

31

43

Scrat Hi

oneyclose Farm

36

44

35

Sweden Sykes

40

Langton Wood

War Meml

96

40

Church Bridge

34

35

LITTLE LANGTON CP

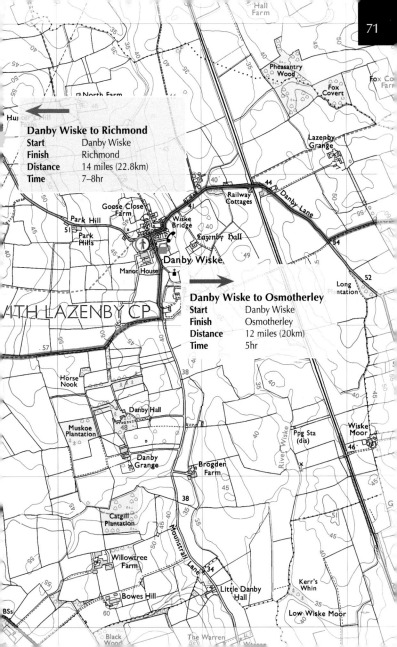

**Danby Wiske to Richmond**

| Start | Danby Wiske |
|---|---|
| Finish | Richmond |
| Distance | 14 miles (22.8km) |
| Time | 7–8hr |

**Danby Wiske to Osmotherley**

| Start | Danby Wiske |
|---|---|
| Finish | Osmotherley |
| Distance | 12 miles (20km) |
| Time | 5hr |

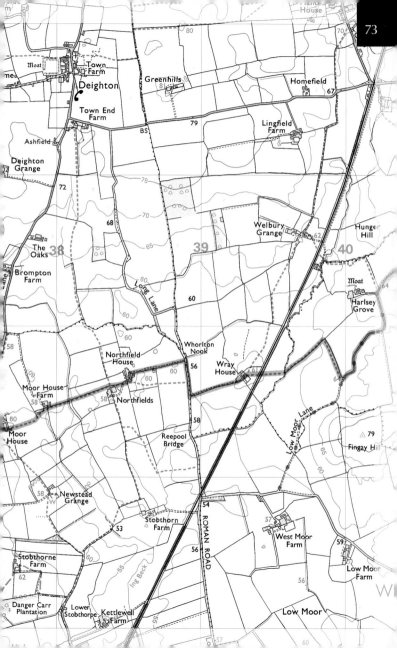

Moat

Town Farm

Deighton

Town End Farm

Greenhills

Homefield

Ashfield

BS

79

Lingfield Farm

Deighton Grange

72

75

68

70

Welbury Grange

62

Hunger Hill

The Oaks

38

65

39

40

Brompton Farm

60

Long Lane

60

Moat

Harlsey Grove

64

60

60

58

60

Whorlton Nook

Wray House

61

Northfield House

60

56

Moor House Farm

58

60

Northfields

Low Moor Lane

Moor House

60

58

Reepool Bridge

79

Fingay Hill

60

Newstead Grange

58

54

57

West Moor Farm

59

53

Stobthorn Farm

ROMAN ROAD

Low Moor Farm

Stobthorne Farm

62

56

56

Danger Carr Plantation

Lower Stobthorpe

Kettlewell Farm

Ing Beck

Low Moor

W

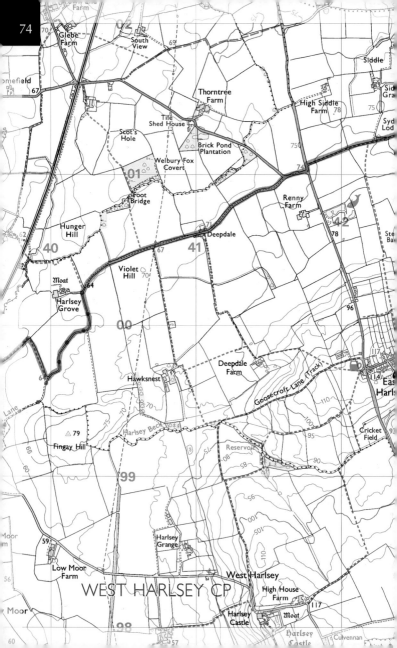

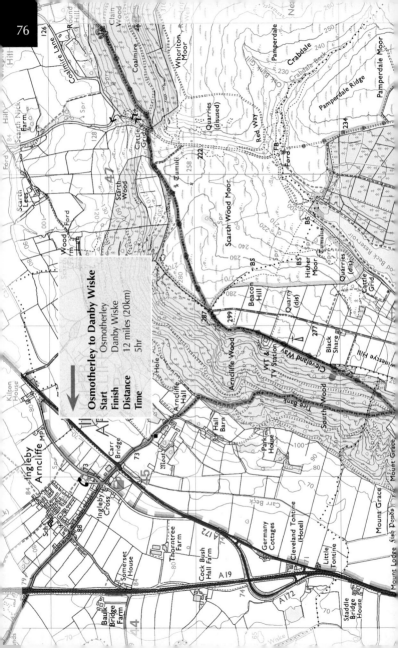

**Osmotherley to Danby Wiske**

| Start | Osmotherley |
|---|---|
| Finish | Danby Wiske |
| Distance | 12 miles (20km) |
| Time | 5hr |

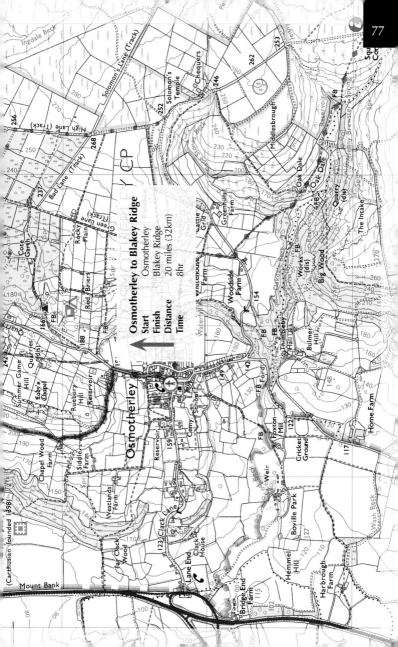

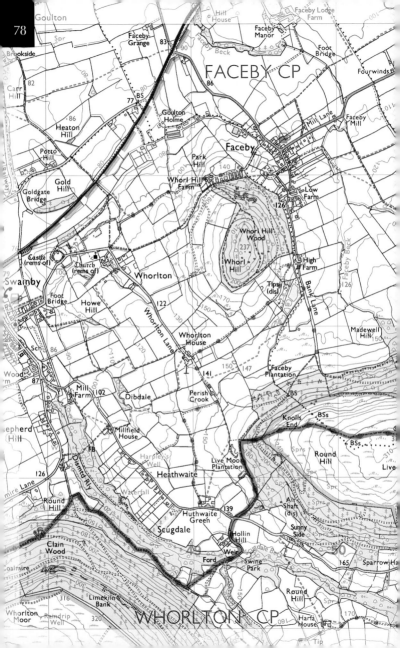

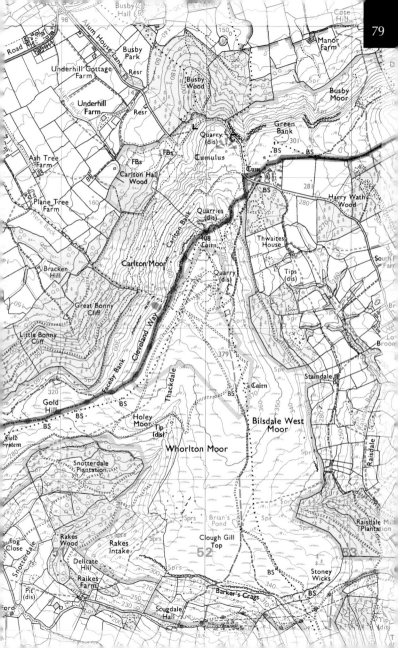

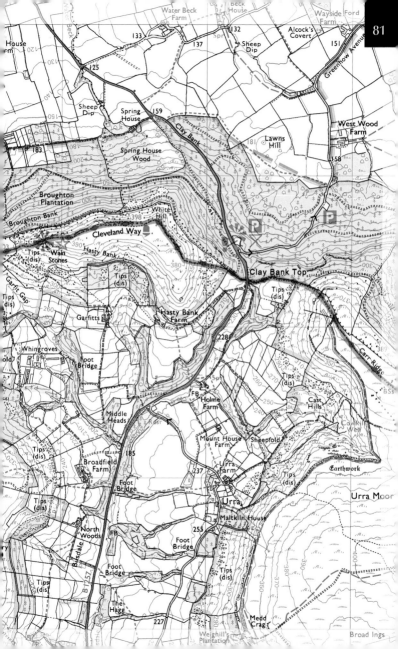

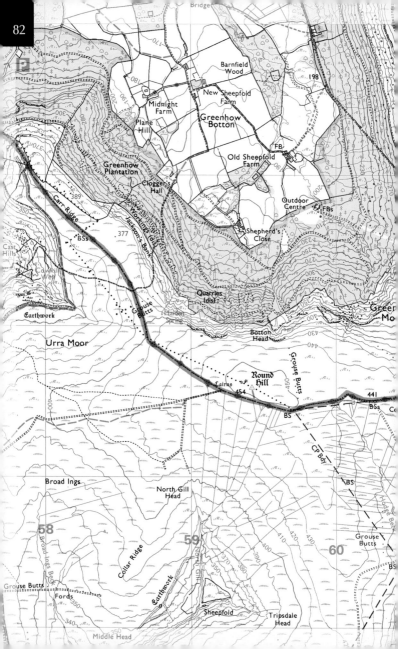

Cl

Butts

BSs Middle Head Top

The Flagged Road (Track)

Workings
(disused)

Armouth
Wath

Grouse
Butts

Stock

Tumuli Burton
Howe

Grouse
Butts

Black Hagg Beck

Quarry
(dis)

Stony Rid

· 434

Incline
Top

432

Grouse Butts

d Scar

415

BSs

420

· 380
· 400
· 420
· 360

Cross
(remains of)

420

421

Grouse
Butts

· 414

Cleveland Way

Low Bloworth

Bloworth
Crossing

High Bloworth

Middle Head

Grouse
Butts

Bransdale

BSs

402

Grouse Butts

61

62

63

· 420
· 410
· 400
· 430

Cockayne Ridge

· 410

398

· 410

Cammon
Stone

Grouse
Butts

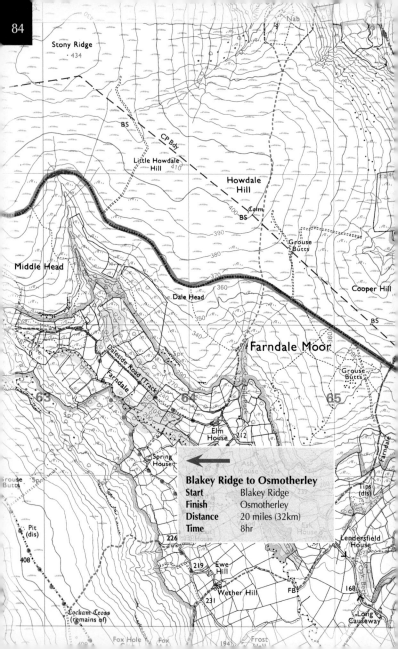

Stony Ridge
· 434

BS

CP Bdy

Little Howdale
Hill          410

Howdale
Hill

Cairn
BS

Middle Head

Grouse
Butts

Cooper Hill

Dale Head

BS

Farndale Moor

Dateside Road (Track)

Farndale

63          64          65

Grouse
Butts

Elm
House          212

Ash
House

Spring
House

**Blakey Ridge to Osmotherley**
**Start**      Blakey Ridge
**Finish**     Osmotherley
**Distance**   20 miles (32km)
**Time**       8hr

Farndale

Tips
(dis)

Grouse
Butts

Pit
(dis)

408

226

Lendersfield
House

219      Ewe
Hill

Wether Hill

231

FB

168

Cockam Cross
(remains of)

Long
Causeway

Fox Hole    Fox          Frost

1941

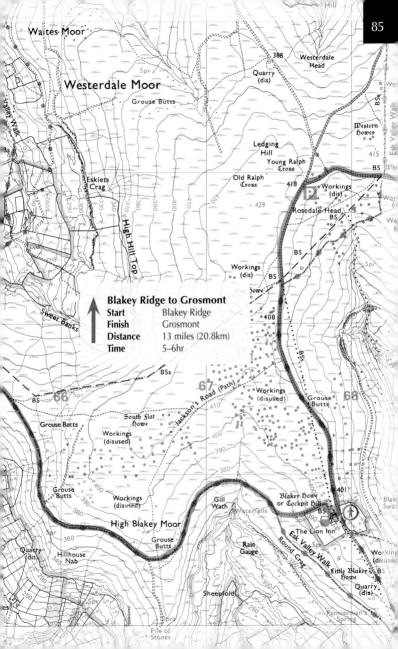

**Blakey Ridge to Grosmont**

| | |
|---|---|
| **Start** | Blakey Ridge |
| **Finish** | Grosmont |
| **Distance** | 13 miles (20.8km) |
| **Time** | 5–6hr |

Waites Moor

Westerdale Moor

Grouse Butts

Valley Walk

Esklets Crag

High Hill Top

Sweet Banks

388

Quarry (dis)

Westerdale Head

BS

Western Howes

Esk Valley Walk

Ledging Hill

Young Ralph Cross

Old Ralph Cross

415

BS

418

P

Workings (dis)

429

Rosedale Head

BS

BS

Workings (dis)

BS

Slat Howe

408

BS

BSs

67

Jackson's Road (Path)

56

Spr

BS

Grouse Butts

South Slat Howe

Workings (disused)

410

Workings (disused)

Grouse Butts

68

400

390

380

Grouse Butts

Workings (disused)

High Blakey Moor

400

390

380

Gill Wath

Waterfalls

Blakey Howe or Cockpit Hill

401

390

The Lion Inn

Esk Valley Walk

Round Crag

Quarry (dis)

Hillhouse Nab

360

Grouse Butts

Rain Gauge

320

Little Blakey Howe

Quarry (dis)

250

Sheepfold

Spr

Pannierman's Spring

Pile of Stones

High Stone Dyke

High Crag

Quarry (dis)

Botton Hall

Botton

Falcon Farm

Resr

Nook House Farm

St Helena

High Farm

Danby Head

Dalehead

Grouse Butts

Honey Bee Nest

Grey Stones

Grouse Butts

Cairn

Stone Rook Hill

372

Quarry (dis)

sterdale Head

Spr

Burnt Rigg

Workings (dis)

Spr

Western Howes

Workings (dis)

Danby High Moor

415

Esk Valley Walk

BSs

Grouse Butts

Workings (dis)

BS White Cross

Danby Head

Botton Cross (remains of)

Trough House

Workings (dis)

Workings (dis)

dale Head, BS

Workings (dis)

CP Bdy

406

423

Wether Hill

Seavey Hill

Gr Be

BSs

Workings (dis)

Spr

415

Mon

P

432

Workings (disused)

BSs

430

Grouse Butts

415

Loose Howe

68

Rosedale

69

Quarries (dis)

Sturdy Bank

70

Quarries (dis)

404

Grouse Butts

Dale Head

Grouse Butts

401

Workings (dis)

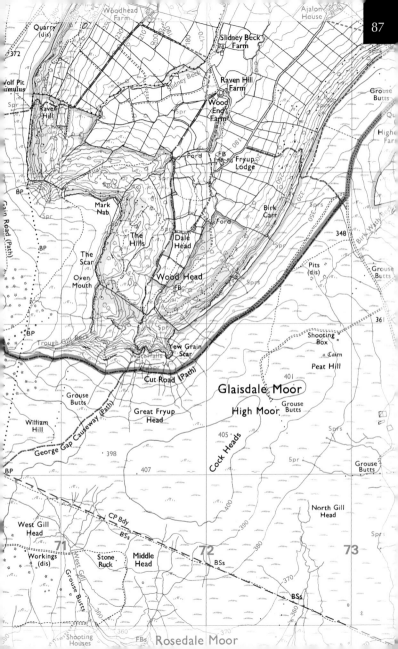

Woodhead Farm
Ajalon House
Quarry (dis)
210
200
Slidney Beck Farm
180
170
372
Raven Hill Farm
Wolf Pit Tumulus
Grouse Butts
Spr
Raven Hill
Wood End Farm
Highe Farm
Spr
Slidney Beck
Spr
Ford
FB
Fryup Lodge
BP
Mark Nab
Spr
180
Birk Carr
Spr
348
Birk Wythe
Ford
The Hills
Dale Head
BP
350
The Scar
Oven Mouth
Wood Head
FB
Spr
Pits (dis)
Grouse Butts
BP
Spr
361
Trough Gill
Yew Grain Scar
Waterfalls
Shooting Box
Cairn
Cut Road (Path)
Peat Hill
BP
401
Grouse Butts
Glaisdale Moor
Great Fryup Head
High Moor
Grouse Butts
William Hill
George Gap Causeway (Path)
405
Cock Heads
398
Spr
BP
407
Grouse Butts
North Gill Head
CP Bdy
BSs
West Gill Head
390
71
72
380
73
Workings (dis)
West Gill
Stone Ruck
Middle Head
BSs
400
370
Grouse Butts
BSs
360
Shooting Houses
FBs
Rosedale Moor
370

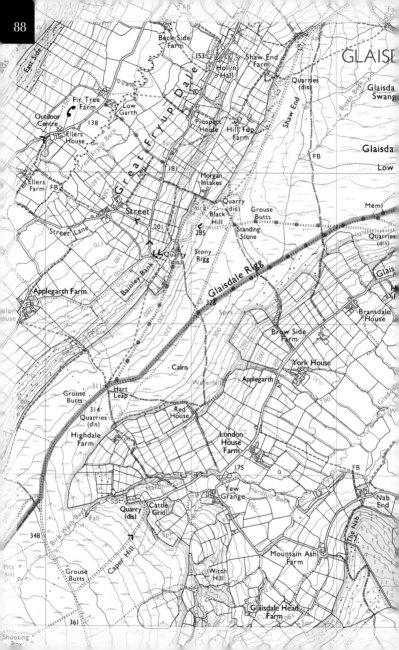

GLAISE

Beck Side Farm

153

Hollin Hall

Shaw End Farm

GLAISE

Quarries (dis)

Glaisda Swang

Fir Tree Farm

Low Garth

Glaisda Low

Outdoor Centre

138

Ellers House

Prospect House

Hill Top Farm

Great Fryup Dale

Shaw End

FB

Great Fryup Beck

181

Morgan Intakes

Ellers Farm FB

Quarry (dis)

Grouse Butts

Meml

Street

201

Black Hill

285

Standing Stone

Quarries (dis)

Street Lane

Quarry (dis)

Stony Rigg

Bagley Bank

Glaisdale Rigg

Glais

Applegarth Farm

326

Brow Side Farm

Bransdale House

York House

Cairn

Waterfall

Applegarth

Grouse Butts

311

Hart Leap

314

Quarries (dis)

Red House

London House Farm

Highdale Farm

175

348

Hardhill Gill

Quarry (dis)

Cattle Grid

Yew Grange

Hardhill Beck

Nab End

Birk Wath Beck

Fall

Caper Hill

Grouse Butts

Mountain Ash Farm

The Nab

Pits (dis)

361

Witch Hill

Glaisdale Head Farm

Shooting Box

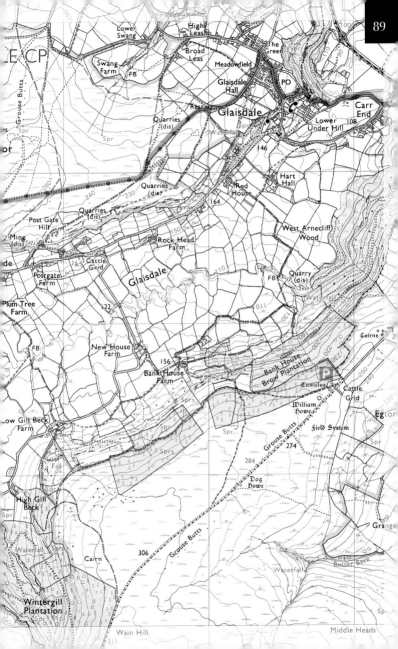

**Grosmont to Robin Hood's Bay**

| | |
|---|---|
| Start | Grosmont |
| Finish | Robin Hood's Bay |
| Distance | 15 miles (24km) |
| Time | 6–7hr |

**Grosmont to Blakey Ridge**

| | |
|---|---|
| Start | Grosmont |
| Finish | Blakey Ridge |
| Distance | 13 miles (20.8km) |
| Time | 5–6hr |

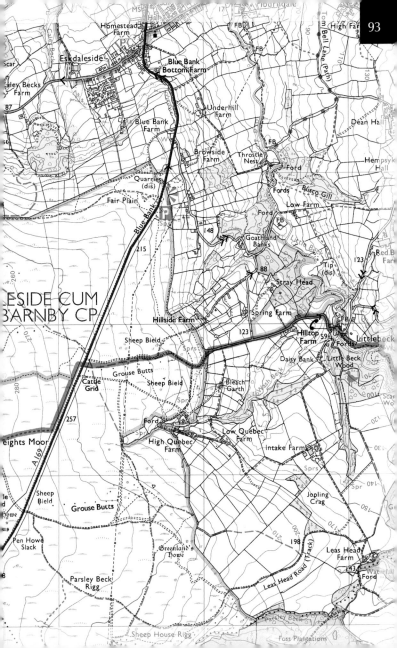

lowe

FB

Maw Wyke
Hole

Pursglove Stye
Batts

Oakham
Wood

Pursglove
Stye

Waterfalls

ms

Ford

Northcliffe
Holiday
Park
108

Limekiln
Slack

Spr

White Stone
Hole

White
Horse

High Scar

Normanby Stye
Batts

Hilda's Howe

Far Jetticks

Clock Case
Nab

Pits
(dis)

Bottom
House    143

Waterfall

Homerell
Hole

Bottom House Lane

Craze
Naze

Rain Dale

T'Awd Abba
Well

Spring Farm

Cow & Calf

Raw Pasture

Spr

Castle
Chamber

Raw Pasture Lane

Spr

Bulmer S

Raw Pasture Bank

163

Bulmer Ste
Hole

176

Smails Moor
Farm

Bay Ness

Ness Point
North Che

High Lane

Quarry
(dis)

Quarry
(dis)

Ness Ruck

by 193

Reservoir

Water

n Hill

Green Hills

**Robin Hood's Bay to Grosmont**

| | |
|---|---|
| **Start** | Robin Hood's Bay |
| **Finish** | Grosmont |
| **Distance** | 15 miles (24km) |
| **Time** | 6–7hr |

## LEGEND OF SYMBOLS
## USED ON ORDNANCE SURVEY
## 1:25,000 (EXPLORER) MAPPING

Map data

### ROADS AND PATHS — Not necessarily rights of way

| | |
|---|---|
| M1 or A6(M) | Motorway — Service Area — Junction Number **7** |
| A 35 | Dual carriageway — Service Area — Toll road junction **T1** |
| A30 | Main road |
| B 3074 | Secondary road |
| | Narrow road with passing places |
| | Road under construction |
| | Road generally more than 4 m wide |
| | Road generally less than 4 m wide |
| | Other road, drive or track, fenced and unfenced |
| | Gradient: steeper than 20% (1 in 5); 14% (1 in 7) to 20% (1 in 5) |
| Ferry | Ferry; Ferry P – passenger only |
| | Path |

### RAILWAYS

Multiple track / standard, Single track / gauge

Narrow gauge or Light rapid transit system (LRTS) and station

Road over; road under; level crossing

Cutting; tunnel; embankment

Station, open to passengers; siding

### PUBLIC RIGHTS OF WAY

- - - - - - Footpath
— — — Bridleway
++++++ Byway open to all traffic
+-+-+- Restricted byway

**The representation on this map of any other road, track or path is no evidence of the existence of a right of way**

### ARCHAEOLOGICAL AND HISTORICAL INFORMATION

| | | | | | |
|---|---|---|---|---|---|
| ⁑ | Site of antiquity | VILLA | Roman | ☆ | Visible earthwork |
| ⚔ 1066 | Site of battle (with date) | Castle | Non-Roman | | |

Information provided by English Heritage for England and the Royal Commissions on the Ancient and Historical Monuments for Scotland and Wales

## HEIGHTS AND NATURAL FEATURES   (continued)

Vertical face/cliff

Loose rock    Boulders    Outcrop    Scree

75
60
50

Contours are at 5 or 10 metre vertical intervals

Water

Mud

Sand; sand and shingle

## SELECTED TOURIST AND LEISURE INFORMATION

Building of historic interest

Cadw

Heritage centre

Camp site

Caravan site

Camping and caravan site

Castle / fort

Cathedral / Abbey

Craft centre

Country park

Cycle trail

Mountain bike trail

Cycle hire

English Heritage

Fishing

Forestry Commission Visitor centre

Garden / arboretum

Golf course or links

Historic Scotland

Information centre, all year

Information centre, seasonal

Horse riding

Museum

National Park Visitor Centre (park logo) e.g. Yorkshire Dales

Nature reserve

National Trust

Other tourist feature

Parking

Park and ride, all year

Park and ride, seasonal

Picnic site

Preserved railway

Public Convenience

Public house/s

Recreation / leisure / sports centre

Roman site (Hadrian's Wall only)

Slipway

Telephone, emergency

Telephone, public

Telephone, roadside assistance

Theme / pleasure park

Viewpoint

Visitor centre

Walks / trails

World Heritage site / area

Water activites

Boat trips

Boat hire

(For complete legend and symbols, see any OS Explorer map).

## OTHER PUBLIC ACCESS

|   |   |   |
|---|---|---|
| • • • | Other routes with public access | The exact nature of the rights on these routes and the existence of any restrictions may be checked with the local highway authority. Alignments are based on the best information available |
| ◆ ◆ ◆ | Recreational route | |
| ◆ ◆ ◆ | 🚶 National Trail    〈⚡〉 Long Distance Route | |
| - - - - - - - - - | Permissive footpath | Footpaths and bridleways along which landowners have permitted public use but which are not rights of way. The agreement may be withdrawn |
| — — — — | Permissive bridleway | |
| • • • | Traffic-free cycle route | |
| 1  **1** | National cycle network  route number – traffic free; on road | |

## ACCESS LAND

 Firing and test ranges in the area. Danger! Observe warning notices

 Access permitted within managed controls, for example, local byelaws. Visit **www.access.mod.uk** for information

### England and Wales

 Access land boundary and tint

Access land in wooded area

 Access information point

Portrayal of access land on this map is intended as a guide to land which is normally available for access on foot, for example access land created under the Countryside and Rights of Way Act 2000, and land managed by the National Trust, Forestry Commission and Woodland Trust. Access for other activities may also exist. Some restrictions will apply; some land will be excluded from open access rights. The depiction of rights of access does not imply or express any warranty as to its accuracy or completeness. Observe local signs and follow the Countryside Code. Visit **www.countrysideaccess.gov.uk** for up-to-date information

## BOUNDARIES

| | |
|---|---|
| — + — + | National |
| — · — · — | County (England) |
| — — — — | Unitary Authority (UA), Metropolitan District (Met Dist), London Borough (LB) or District (Scotland & Wales are solely Unitary Authorities) |
| · · · · · · · · · · | Civil Parish (CP) (England) or Community (C) (Wales) |
|  | National Park boundary |

## VEGETATION

Limits of vegetation are defined by positioning of symbols

| | |
|---|---|
| 🌲 | Coniferous trees |
| 🌳 | Non-coniferous trees |
| | Coppice |
| ° ° ° | Orchard |
| | Scrub |
| | Bracken, heath or rough grassland |
| | Marsh, reeds or saltings |

## HEIGHTS AND NATURAL FEATURES

| | | |
|---|---|---|
| 52 · | Ground survey height | Surface heights are to the nearest metre above mean sea level. Where two heights are shown, the first height is to the base of the triangulation pillar and the second (in brackets) to the highest natural point of the hill |
| 284 · | Air survey height | |

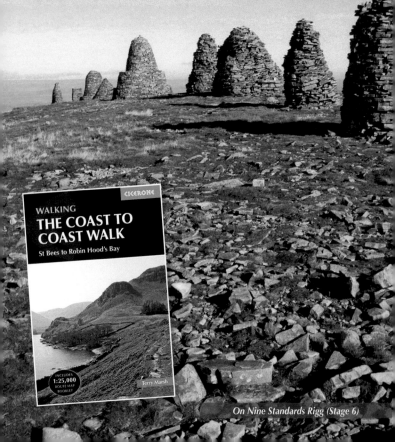

# THE COAST TO COAST WALK

This map booklet accompanies the latest edition of Terry Marsh's guidebook to the Coast to Coast Walk, described principally from west to east (with summary route description east to west), between St Bees Head and Robin Hood's Bay. The guidebook features annotated 1:100,000 mapping alongside detailed step-by-step route description, with lots of planning advice and other information about local history, geography and wildlife.

CICERONE

WALKING
## THE COAST TO COAST WALK
St Bees to Robin Hood's Bay

INCLUDES 1:25,000 ROUTE MAP BOOKLET

Terry Marsh

*On Nine Standards Rigg (Stage 6)*

# OTHER CICERONE TRAIL GUIDES

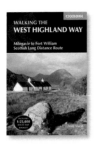
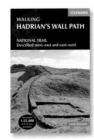
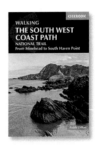
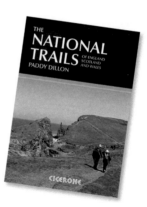